Handy Missouri Genealogy Handbook

I0450183

By Gary L. Morris

©2015 Gary L. Morris

ISBN-13: 978-1507722077

ISBN-10: 1507722079

Table of Contents

Notes

Genealogical Research in Missouri

Tracing your family history in Missouri can be a fascinating trip
through time. Exciting characters like Kit Carson, Jesse James,
former President Harry S. Truman, and the gifted Walt Disney all
hail from Missouri. As one of the earliest areas in America settled by
Europeans, there are a wealth of genealogical records and resources
for tracing your family history in Missouri. Tracking these records
down can be an ominous task, but don't worry, we know just where
they are, and we'll show you which records you'll need, and help
you to understand:

1.   What they are
2.   Where to find them
3.   How to use them

These records can be found both online and off, so we'll introduce
you to online websites, indexes and databases, as well as brick-and-
mortar repositories and other institutions that will help with your
research in Missouri. So that you will have a more comprehensive
understanding of these records, we have provided a brief history of
the "Show Me State" to illustrate what type of records may have
been generated during specific time periods. That information will
assist you in pinpointing times and locations on which to focus the
search for your Missouri ancestors and their records.

A Brief History of Missouri

Missouri takes its name from the Missouri Indians who inhabited the area, but many other tribes including the Miamis, Kickapoos, Sacs, Foxes, Osages, Otos, Iowas, Delawares, Shawnees and Kansas also made their home in the region. The French were the first to explore the area, and La Salle claimed the region for France in 1682. In 1762 the area was ceded to Spain who ruled the region for another forty years.

Lead mining was very much at the forefront of Missouri's early development after as lead ore called Galena was discovered there in 1701. Significant deposits were uncovered and by 1720 mining was in full force, fuelled by the labor of early French settlers. The French established the first official settlement at Ste. Genevieve in the mid 1730s, and it was the sole settlement for around thirty years until a trading post was established at St. Louis in 1764.

Spain ceded the Louisiana Territory back to France in 1802, and Missouri was sold as part of that to the United States in the Louisiana Purchase the following year. In 1804 the famous Lewis and Clarke expedition set sail from St. Louis. In 1812 Missouri was organized as a separate territory and became a state in 1821.

Missouri had become a slave state with the passing of the Missouri Compromise in 1820, but its loyalty remained with the Union cause during the Civil War. This was in spite of the attempts by governor Claiborne Fox Jackson to align Missouri with the Confederacy due to his personal ties to the South. Eventually Jackson and most of his legislature were forced to flee the state after the majority of Missourians refused to recognize his government. 109,000 men from Missouri fought for the Union, 30,000 for the Confederate side.

Important Dates in Missouri History

1682 – Region claimed for France

1763 – Ceded from France to Spain

1764 – St. Louis founded

1800 – Ceded from Spain to France

1803 – Part of the Louisiana Purchase

1804 – Lewis and Clarke expedition commences from St. Louis

1805 – Part of the Louisiana Territory

1812 – Created as separate territory

1820 – Missouri Compromise makes slavery legal

1820 - Statehood

Famous Battles Fought in Missouri

The bloodiest and most important battle fought in Missouri was the **Battle of Wilson's Creek** near Springfield. Other important conflicts in the state were fought at the **Battle of Carthage**, the **Battle of Lexington**, the **Battle of Westport**, and the **Battle of Boonville** - the first engagement within the state

These battle accounts that do exist can be very effective in uncovering the military records of your ancestor. They can tell you what regiments fought in which battles, and often include the names and ranks of many officers and enlisted men.

Battle of Wilson's Creek:
http://www.civilwar.org/battlefields/wilson-s-creek.html

Battle of Carthage: http://www.mcwm.org/history_battle-of-carthage.html

Battle of Lexington:
http://www.nps.gov/hps/abpp/battles/mo006.htm

Battle of Westport:
http://www.nps.gov/hps/abpp/battles/mo027.htm

Battle of Boonville: http://www.mcwm.org/history_battle-of-boonville.html

Common Missouri Genealogical Issues and Resources to Overcome Them

Boundary Changes: Boundary changes are a common obstacle when researching Missouri ancestors. You could be searching for an ancestor's record in one county when in fact it is stored in a different one due to historical county boundary changes.

The **Atlas of Historical County Boundaries** can help you to overcome that problem. It provides a chronological listing of every boundary change that has occurred in the history of Missouri.

Atlas of Historical County Boundaries:
http://publications.newberry.org/ahcbp/documents/MO_Consolidate
d_Chronology.htm#Consolidated_Chronology

Name Changes: Surname changes, variations, and misspellings can complicate genealogical research. It is important to check all spelling variations. Soundex, a program that indexes names by sound, is a useful first step, but you can't rely on it completely as some name variations result in different Soundex codes. The surnames could be different, but the first name may be different too. You can also find records filed under initials, middle names, and nicknames as well, so you will need to **get creative with surname variations** and spellings in order to cover all the possibilities. For help with surname variations read our instructional article on **How to Use Soundex**.

get creative with surname variations:
http://obituarieshelp.org/blog/?p=634

How to Use Soundex: http://obituarieshelp.org/blog/?p=505

Missouri Genealogical Organizations and Archives

Genealogical resources include not only records, but the organizations that house them, or can direct you to them. These institutions include: *Archives, Libraries, Genealogical Societies, Family History Centers, Universities, Churches, and Museums.*

Following are links to their websites, their physical addresses, and a summary of the records you can find there.

Archives and Libraries

Missouri State Archives – pre 1910 vital records database, Civil War Provost Marshall Index, county records (deeds, marriages, circuit court and probate court materials), municipal records, Coroner's Inquest database, Land Patents database, census records, judicial records, probate records, military records (War of 1812, Mexican War, Spanish American War, and WWI), naturalization records, and many other local and state records

600 West Main Street
Jefferson City, MO 65101
Phone: (573) 751-3280

Missouri State Archives:
http://www.sos.mo.gov/archives/resources/ordb.asp

National Archives at Kansas City – census records, military records, pension and bounty-land warrant applications, historical newspapers, surnames index, gazetteer

400 West Pershing Road
Kansas City, MO 64108
Phone: 816-268-8000
E-mail: kansascity.archives@nara.gov

National Archives at Kansas City:
http://www.archives.gov/kansas-city/public/

Kansas City Public Library – census indexes and genealogy material covering the states from which Missouri residents emigrated

Missouri Valley Special Collections
14 W. 10th Street
Kansas City, MO 64105
Voice: (816) 701-3427
E-mail: lhistory@kclibrary.org

Kansas City Public Library: http://www.kclibrary.org/kchistory

Harry S. Truman Library and Museum – personal papers, oral histories, historical photographs and documents

500 W. US Hwy. 24.
Independence MO 64050
Tel: 816-268-8200 or 1-800-833-1225
Fax: 816-268-8295
E-mail: truman.library@nara.gov

Harry S. Truman Library and Museum:
http://www.trumanlibrary.org/

Missouri Genealogical and Historical Societies

Genealogical and historical societies have access to extensive catalogues of genealogical data. They are also able to offer expert guidance for genealogical researchers. Many members are professional genealogists who are most willing to share their expertise in finding ancestors.

State Historical Society of Missouri - census records, historical maps, historical newspapers, manuscripts, oral histories and more

1020 Lowry Street
Columbia, Missouri 65201-7298
Toll Free: (800) 747-6366 or (573) 882-7083
Fax: (573) 884-4950

State Historical Society of Missouri:
http://shs.umsystem.edu/index.shtml

Missouri State Genealogical Association – surname index and many genealogical resources for searching newspapers, cemeteries, church records, immigration records, military records, and more

Missouri State Genealogical Association
P.O. Box 833
Columbia, MO 65205-0833
Email: webmanager@mosga.org

Missouri State Genealogical Association:
http://mosga.org/cpage.php?pt=16

Midwest Genealogy Center – original family histories, military records, land records, photographs, and more

Midwest Genealogy Center link to:
http://www.mymcpl.org/genealogy/resources-genealogy-family-history

Genealogical Society of Central Missouri - Cemetery/Tombstone Records - 1821-1870, Marriage Records - 1821-1870, Land ownership Maps - 1875, 1898, 1917, 1976, 1979, Histories - all known published histories of Boone County, Biographies, City Directories

Genealogical Society of Central Missouri
P.O. Box 26
Columbia, MO 65205-0026
Email: gscm75@gmail.com

Library Address:

Wilson-Wulff Genealogy-History Library
Walters-Boone County Historical Society Museum
3801 Ponderosa Drive
Columbia, MO   65201

Genealogical Society of Central Missouri:
http://gscm.missouri.org/facilities.html

St. Louis Genealogical Society – variety of St. Louis genealogy records, research services, genealogy library

St. Louis Genealogical Society
#4 Sunnen Drive, Suite 140
St. Louis, MO 63143
By Mail:
St. Louis Genealogical Society
P.O. Box 432010
St. Louis, MO 63143

Tel: 314-647-8547
Fax: 314-647-8548
Email:office@stlgs.org
Website: http://stlgs.org/

Additional Missouri Genealogical Resources

<u>Missouri Mailing Lists</u>

Mailing lists are internet based facilities that use email to distribute a single message to all who subscribe to it. When information on a particular surname, new records, or any other important genealogy information related to the mailing list topic becomes available, the subscribers are alerted to it. Joining a mailing list is an excellent way to stay up to date on Missouri genealogy research topics. Rootsweb have an extensive listing of **Missouri Mailing Lists** on a variety of topics.

Missouri Mailing Lists:
http://lists.rootsweb.ancestry.com/index/usa/MO/misc.html

<u>Missouri Message Boards</u>

A message board is another internet based facility where people can post questions about a specific genealogy topic and have it answered by other genealogists. If you have questions about a surname, record type, or research topic, you can post your question and other researchers and genealogists will help you with the answer. Be sure to check back regularly, as the answers are not emailed to you. The Missouri message boards at the **Rootsweb** are completely free to use.

Rootsweb:
http://boards.rootsweb.com/localities.northam.usa.states/mb.ashx

Missouri Newspapers and Periodicals

Many genealogy periodicals and historical newspapers contain reprinted copies of family genealogies, transcripts of family Bible records, information about local records and archives, census indexes, church records, queries, land records, obituaries, court records, cemetery records, and wills. The following sites have historical Missouri newspapers and periodicals that you can search online or on-site.

State Historical Society of Missouri - over forty-one million newspaper pages of microfilm beginning with the July 26, 1808, issue of the St. Louis Missouri Gazette

1020 Lowry Street
Columbia, Missouri 65201-7298
Toll Free: (800) 747-6366 or (573) 882-7083
Fax: (573) 884-4950

State Historical Society of Missouri:
http://shs.umsystem.edu/index.shtml

GenealogyBank.com – free searchable database of Missouri newspaper archives, 1808–1949

GenealogyBank.com :
http://www.genealogybank.com/gbnk/newspapers/explore/USA/Missouri/

Library of Congress Digital Newspaper Directory – free searchable database of historical U.S. newspapers dating from 1690-present

Library of Congress Digital Newspaper Directory:
http://chroniclingamerica.loc.gov/search/titles/

The Online Books Page – links to historical Missouri books and periodicals available for viewing online, dating from mid-16th century

The Online Books Page: http://onlinebooks.library.upenn.edu

NewspaperArchive.com – largest online database of historical newspapers in the world.

NewspaperArchive.com: http://newspaperarchive.com/

Historical Missouri Maps and Gazetteers

Maps are an integral part of genealogical research. They help us to locate landmarks, towns, cities, parishes, states, provinces, waterways and roads and streets. They also help us to determine when and where boundary changes might have taken place, and give us a visualization of the area we're researching in.

For locating place names, a gazetteer is the best possible resource for any genealogist. Gazetteers are also sometimes called "place name dictionaries", and can help you to locate the area in which you need to conduct research. Below are links to the maps and gazetteers for research in Missouri.

Peabody GNIS Service – Missouri:
http://peabody.research.yale.edu/cgi-bin/Query.GNIS?ST=Missouri&SU=1

Color Landform Atlas – Missouri:
http://fermi.jhuapl.edu/states/mo_0.html

1985 U.S. Atlas: http://www.livgenmi.com/1895/MO/

Missouri Hometown Locator:
http://missouri.hometownlocator.com/

Missouri City Directories
.

City directories are similar to telephone directories in that they list the residents of a particular area. The difference though is what is important to genealogists, and that is they pre-date telephone directories. You can find an ancestor's information such as their street address, place of employment, occupation, or the name of their spouse. A one-stop-shop for finding city directories in Missouri is the **Missouri Online Historical Directories** which contains a listing of every available online historical directory related to Missouri.

Missouri Online Historical Directories:
https://sites.google.com/site/onlinedirectorysite/Home/usa/mo

Missouri History Museum – St. Louis City directories from 1821 to 1980 and St. Louis County directories from 1893 to 1979.

P.O. Box 11940
St. Louis, MO 63112
Tel: (314) 746-4599

Missouri History Museum: http://mohistory.org/node/7172

Missouri Genealogical Records

<u>Birth, Death, Marriage and Divorce Records</u> – Also known as vital records, birth, death, and marriage certificates are the most basic, yet most important records attached to your ancestor. The reason for their importance is that they not only place your ancestor in a specific place at a definite time, but potentially connect the individual to other relatives. Below is a list of repositories and websites where you can find Missouri vital records.

Bureau of Vital Records – birth and death records from 1910 to present, marriage and divorce records from 1948 to present

Missouri Department of Health and Senior Services
P.O. Box 570
Jefferson City, MO 65102
Tel: 573-751-6387
Email:VitalRecordsInfo@health.mo.gov

Bureau of Vital Records: http://health.mo.gov/data/vitalrecords/

Missouri State Archives – birth, stillbirth, and death records recorded before 1909, Death certificates, 1910-1962, marriage records and index, marriage applications, African American marriage records, register of marriage licenses, divorce records

600 West Main Street
Jefferson City, MO 65101
Phone: (573) 751-3280

Missouri State Archives:
http://www.sos.mo.gov/archives/resources/ordb.asp

Genealogical Society of Central Missouri - Cemetery/Tombstone Records - 1821-1870, Marriage Records - 1821-1870, 1821-1915

Genealogical Society of Central Missouri
P.O. Box 26
Columbia, MO 65205-0026
Email: gscm75@gmail.com
Library Address:

Wilson-Wulff Genealogy-History Library
Walters-Boone County Historical Society Museum
3801 Ponderosa Drive
Columbia, MO   65201

Genealogical Society of Central Missouri:
http://gscm.missouri.org/facilities.html

Family Search has the following indexes which can be searched online for free:

Missouri Births and Christenings, 1827-1935:
https://familysearch.org/search/collection/1680833

Missouri County Marriage Records, 1819-1969:
https://familysearch.org/search/collection/2060668

Missouri Deaths and Burials, 1867-1976:
https://familysearch.org/search/collection/1680837

Census Reports

Census records are among the most important genealogical documents for placing your ancestor in a particular place at a specific time. Like BDM records, they can also lead you to other ancestors, particularly those who were living under the authority of the head of household.

Federal census records for Missouri exist from 1790–1930 and can be found at:

National Archives at Kansas City – Federal population censuses for all States, 1790-1930, indexes for the 1880, 1900, 1910, and 1920 censuses, censuses and land allotment files for Native Americans

400 West Pershing Road
Kansas City, MO 64108
Phone: 816-268-8000
E-mail: kansascity.archives@nara.gov

National Archives at Kansas City:
http://www.archives.gov/kansas-city/public/

Missouri State Archives – census records for the years 1830 through 1930, with the exception of the 1890 census which was destroyed by fire, Special Veterans Census for 1890

600 West Main Street
Jefferson City, MO 65101
Phone: (573) 751-3280

Missouri State Archives:
http://www.sos.mo.gov/archives/resources/ordb.asp

The **Free Census Project** has transcribed many Missouri indexes and new material is added daily

Free Census Project: http://usgwcensus.org/cenfiles/mo.htm

Access Genealogy – Missouri county census records from 1850-1930

Access Genealogy:
http://www.accessgenealogy.com/census/missouri-census-records.htm

African American Census Schedules Online – slave schedules, mortality schedules, slave-owners census

African American Census Schedules Online:
http://www.afrigeneas.com/aacensus/ga/

Native Americans in Census Records (US National Archives):
http://www.archives.gov/research/census/native-americans/

Missouri Church Records

Church and synagogue records are a valuable resource, especially for baptisms, marriages, and burials that took place before 1900. You will need to at least have an idea of your ancestor's religious denomination, and in most cases you will have to visit a brick and mortar establishment to view them.

Most church records are kept by the individual church, although in some denominations, records are placed in a regional archive or maintained at the diocesan level. Local Historical Societies are sometimes the repository for the state's older church records. Below are links archives that maintain church records, as well as a few databases that can be viewed online.

The **Family History Library** contains many church records from a variety of denominations on microfilm.

Family History Library:
http://familysearch.org/learn/wiki/en/Family_History_Library

Central Repositories for Denominational Records

State Historical Society of Missouri – Baptist, Catholic, Church of Christ, Church of the Messiah, Episcopal, Evangelical, Protestant, Jewish, Lutheran, Methodist, Mormon, and Presbyterian records dating from early 19th century. Collection consists of newsletters, minutes, conference proceedings, reports, directories, journals, and other publications

1020 Lowry Street
Columbia, Missouri 65201-7298
Toll Free: (800) 747-6366 or (573) 882-7083
Fax: (573) 884-4950

State Historical Society of Missouri:
http://shs.umsystem.edu/manuscripts/invent/0558.pdf

Swenson Center, Augustana College – Baptist, Lutheran, First Covenant, and Scandinavian Union records

Swenson Center, Augustana College:
https://www.augustana.edu/general-information/swenson-center-/genealogy/church-records/missouri---oregon

St. Charles County Historical Society – Huge inventory of church records from multiple denominations including Catholic, Lutheran, Methodist, Evangelical, Episcopal, and African Methodist. Record types include Baptisms, Marriages, Burials, and member's lists

101 South Main
St. Charles, Missouri
Email: contact via online form

St. Charles County Historical Society:
http://scchs.org/research/indexes/church-record.html

If you don't find your ancestors records using the above sources you'll have to search in brick and mortar establishments. Most of the records of individual denominations are kept in central repositories. Below is a list of the major congregational archives for Missouri with links to their websites, physical addresses, and contact information.

Baptist

Southern Baptist Historical Library and Archives
901 Commerce Street, Suite 400
Nashville, TN 37203-3630
Phone: (615) 244-0344
Fax: (615) 782-4821

Southern Baptist Historical Library and Archives:
http://www.sbhla.org/

Missouri Baptist Historical Commission
400 East High Street
Jefferson City, Missouri 65101
Phone: (573) 636-0400 ext. 371/ Toll Free: (800) 736-6227 ext. 371

Missouri Baptist Historical Commission:
http://baptistparchments.org/

Missouri Baptist Historical Society
William Jewell College
500 College Hill
Liberty, MO 64068
Phone: (816) 781-7700 ext.5468
Fax: (816) 415-5027

Missouri Baptist Historical Society:
http://www.jewell.edu/gen/william_and_jewell_generated_pages/Mi
ssouri_Baptist_Historical_Society_p1845.html

American Baptist Historical Society
1106 South Goodman Street
Rochester, NY 14620-2532
Phone: (716) 473-1740

American Baptist Historical Society: bhsarchives.org

Disciples of Christ

Disciples of Christ Historical Society
1101 19th Avenue S
Nashville, TN 37212-2196
Phone: (615) 327-1444
Fax: (615) 327-1445

Disciples of Christ Historical Society:
http://www.discipleshistory.org/

Church of Jesus Christ of Latter-day Saints (Mormons)

Early Mormon Church records for Missouri can be found on film located at the LDS Family History Library in Salt Lake City and can be searched via the **Family History Library Catalog**

Family History Library Catalog:
https://familysearch.org/eng/Library/FHLC/frameset_fhlc.asp

Lutheran

A large collection of online records, indexes, and church histories can be found at the Genealoger website's **Lutheran Genealogy Missouri Lutheran Church Records & Histories** page.

Lutheran Genealogy Missouri Lutheran Church Records & Histories:
http://www.genealoger.com/lutheran/church%20records/luth_chrec_missouri.htm

Methodist

United Methodist Church Archives
411 Central Methodist Square
Fayette, MO 65248
Phone: (816) 248-3391 ext. 292
Fax: (816) 248-3045

United Methodist Church Archives:
http://www.gcah.org/site/c.ghKJI0PHIoE/b.2858857/k.BF4D/Home.htm

Roman Catholic

Diocese of Kansas City-St. Joseph
300 East 36th
Kansas City, MO 64111
Phone: (816) 756-1850

Mailing Address
P.O. Box 419037
Kansas City, MO 64141-6037

Diocese of Kansas City-St. Joseph: http://www.diocese-kcsj.org/content/diocese/archives/

Diocese of Springfield-Cape Girardeau
601 S. Jefferson Ave.
Springfield, MO 65806
Phone: (417) 866-0841

Diocese of Springfield-Cape Girardeau: http://www.dioscg.org/

Archdiocese of St. Louis
4445 Lindell Boulevard
St. Louis, MO 63108-2497
Phone: (314) 533-1887
Fax: (314) 533-1889

Archdiocese of St. Louis: http://archstl.org/archives

Missouri Military Records

More than 40 million Americans have participated in some time of war service since America was colonized. The chance of finding your ancestor amongst those records is exceptionally high. Military records can even reveal individuals who never actually served, such as those who registered for the two World Wars but were never called to duty.

Below are a number of links to websites and archives that contain Missouri military records.

Missouri State Archives – pre 1910 vital records database, Civil War Provost Marshall Index, War of 1812, Mexican War, Spanish American War, and WWI records

600 West Main Street
Jefferson City, MO 65101
Phone: (573) 751-3280

Missouri State Archives:
http://www.sos.mo.gov/archives/resources/ordb.asp

National Archives at Kansas City – selected military service records and indexes; selected pension and bounty-land warrant applications

400 West Pershing Road
Kansas City, MO 64108
Phone: 816-268-8000
E-mail: kansascity.archives@nara.gov

National Archives at Kansas City:
http://www.archives.gov/kansas-city/public/

U.S. National Archives – WWI Draft registration cards, casualties lists, WWI and WWII service records, Korean War records, Vietnam War records, Civil War and Spanish-American War records, and casualties lists.

U.S. National Archives: http://www.archives.gov/research/military/veterans/online.html

US Department of Veterans Affairs Nationwide Gravesite Locator – includes information on veterans and their family members buried in veterans and military cemeteries having a government grave marker.

US Department of Veterans Affairs Nationwide Gravesite Locator: http://gravelocator.cem.va.gov/

You may also find your ancestor's military records in the following databases:

Missouri Civil War Service Records of Confederate Soldiers, 1861-1865: https://familysearch.org/search/collection/1932374

United States General Index to Pension Files, 1861-1934: https://familysearch.org/search/collection/1919699

United States Index to Service Records, War with Spain, 1898: https://familysearch.org/search/collection/1919583

United States Index to Indian Wars Pension Files, 1892-1926 – military pension records of soldiers who fought in the Indian Wars between 1817 and 1898

United States Index to Indian Wars Pension Files, 1892-1926: https://familysearch.org/search/collection/1979427

United States Registers of Enlistments in the U.S. Army, 1798-1914 - index of men who enlisted in the United States Army, 1798-1914.

United States Registers of Enlistments in the U.S. Army, 1798-1914: https://familysearch.org/search/collection/1880762

United States Mexican War Pension Index, 1887-1926 - index to Mexican War pension files for service between 1846 and 1848

United States Mexican War Pension Index, 1887-1926: https://familysearch.org/search/collection/1979390

Civil War Soldiers Service Records - Service records for both Union and Confederate soldiers indexed by soldier's name, rank, and unit.

Civil War Soldier Service Records: http://go.fold3.com/civilwar_records/

Missouri Cemetery Records

As convenient as it is to search cemetery records online, keep in mind that there are a few disadvantages over visiting a cemetery in person. They are:

- Tombstone information is not always accurately transcribed
- The arrangement of the graves in a cemetery can be crucial as family members are often buried next to each other or in the same grave. This arrangement is not always preserved in the alphabetical indexes that are found online.

With that information in mind, the following websites have databases that can be searched online for Missouri Cemetery records.

Missouri Tombstone Transcription Project - death and burial records

Missouri Tombstone Transcription Project: http://www.usgwtombstones.org/missouri/missouri.html

African American Cemeteries Online – African American, slave, and Native American cemetery records

African American Cemeteries Online: http://africanamericancemeteries.com/ar/

Access Genealogy – huge database of Missouri cemetery record transcriptions

Access Genealogy: http://www.accessgenealogy.com/cemetery/missouri-cemetery-records.htm

Find a Grave – over 100 million grave records can be searched on this site. Search can be conducted by name, location, or cemetery name.

Find a Grave: http://www.findagrave.com/

Interment.net - A free online database containing approximately 4 million cemetery records from around the world.

Interment.net: http://www.interment.net/

Billion Graves – as the name implies, you can search a billion records including headstone photos, transcriptions, cemetery records, and grave locations.

Billion Graves:
http://billiongraves.com/pages/search/index.php#cemetery

Missouri Obituaries

Obituaries can reveal a wealth about our ancestor and other relatives. You can search our **Missouri Newspaper Obituaries Listings** from hundreds of Missouri newspapers online for free.

Missouri Newspaper Obituaries Listings:
http://obituarieshelp.org/missouri_newspaper_obituaries.html

Missouri Wills and Probate Records

The documents found in a probate packet may include a complete inventory of a person's estate, newspaper entries, witness testimony, a copy of a will, list of debtors and creditors, names of executors or trustees, names of heirs. They can not only tell you about the ancestor you're currently researching, but lead to other ancestors.

Missouri State Archives – wills and probate records from every county in Missouri dating from early 19th century

600 West Main Street
Jefferson City, MO 65101
Phone: (573) 751-3280

Missouri State Archives:
http://www.sos.mo.gov/archives/resources/ordb.asp

Family Search has the following indexes that can be searched online for free:

Missouri Cole County Circuit Court Case Files, 1820-1926:
https://familysearch.org/search/collection/2076858

Missouri Probate Records, 1800-1959:
https://familysearch.org/search/collection/2060218

Missouri Immigration and Naturalization Records

The naturalization process generated many types of records, including petitions, declarations of intention, and oaths of allegiance. These records can provide family historians with information such as a person's birth date and place of birth, immigration year, marital status, spouse information, occupation, witnesses' names and addresses, and more.

Missouri State Archives – Naturalization Records, 1816 - 1955

600 West Main Street
Jefferson City, MO 65101
Phone: (573) 751-3280

Missouri State Archives:
http://www.sos.mo.gov/archives/resources/ordb.asp

State Historical Society of Missouri – Immigrant Collection - Personal papers, organizational records, and other materials related to immigrants

1020 Lowry Street
Columbia, Missouri 65201-7298
Toll Free: (800) 747-6366 or (573) 882-7083
Fax: (573) 884-4950

State Historical Society of Missouri:
http://shs.umsystem.edu/manuscripts/descriptions/desc-immigrants.html

Family Search has the following index that can be searched online for free:

Missouri County Naturalization Records, 1883-1927 link to:
https://familysearch.org/search/collection/1880587

Missouri Native American Records

Access Genealogy – Missouri Native American census records, tribal histories, and much more

Access Genealogy: http://www.accessgenealogy.com/native/missouri-indian-tribes.htm

U.S. National Archives - information on American Indians who maintained their ties to Federally-recognized Tribes (1830-1970).

U.S. National Archives: http://www.archives.gov/research/native-americans/

Records of the Bureau of Indian Affairs (BIA): http://www.archives.gov/research/guide-fed-records/groups/075.html

American Indians Records Repository - records dating from the 1700s including trust, education and other historic Indian Affairs records

American Indian Records Repository
Meritex Enterprises
17501 West 98th Street
Lenexa, KS 66219
Phone: 913-888-0601

American Indians Records Repository: http://www.doi.gov/ost/records_mgmt/american-indian-records-repository.cfm

Missing Matriarchs – Resources for Researching Female Missouri Ancestors

Looking for female ancestors requires an adjustment of how we view traditional records sources. A woman's identity was often under that of her husband, and often individual records for them can be difficult to locate. The following resources are effective in locating female ancestors in Missouri where traditional records may not reveal them.

<u>Bibliographies</u>

- *In Her Place: A Guide to St. Louis Women's History, 1764-1965,* Catherine T. Corbett (Missouri Historical Society Press)
- *Show Me Missouri Women, Selected Biographies: Missouri Women's History Project,* Mary K. Dains (Thomas Jefferson University Press)
- *Kansas City Women of Independent Minds,* Jan F. Flynn (Fifield Publishing, 1992)
- *Women of the Earth Lodges: Tribal Life on the Plains,* Virginia B. Peters (Archon Books, 1997)
- *Death Records of Pioneer Missouri Women, 1808-1853,* Lois Stanley (Southern Historical Press, 1990)

Selected Resources for Missouri Women's History

State Historical Society of Missouri Womens Collection
1020 Lowry Street
Columbia, Missouri 65201-7298
Toll Free: (800) 747-6366 or (573) 882-7083
Fax: (573) 884-4950

Blanche Skiff Ross Memorial Library
Cottey College
225 South College
Nevada, MO 64772

Common Missouri Surnames

The following surnames are among the most common in Missouri and are also being currently researched by other genealogists. If you find your surname here, there is a chance that some research has already been performed on your ancestor.

Aaron, Abbott, Adair, Adams, Adamson, Adcock, Adkins, Aiken, Ainsworth, Akin, Aldridge, Alexander, Alford, Alfrey, Alger, Allen, Allison, Alspach, Amos, Anders, Anderson, Andress, Andrews, Andrus, Anjou, Apple, Archer, Armstrong, Ashton, Ashworth, Atkinson, Atwood, Austin, Avery, Ayers, Babb, Bailey, Baker, Baldwin, Barber, Barnett, Barnhart, Barrett, Barrow, Barton, Bass, Bateman, Batson, Baughman, Beatty, Bell, Bennett, Benningfield, Berry, Black, Black Cloud, Block, Boling, Booth, Born, Boyd, Bradley, Brady, Bright, Brooks, Brown, Buck, Bumstead, Burch, Burgundy, Burns, Butler, Byerly, Byrd, Cain, Campbell, Cardwell, Carr, Carroll, Carter, Caudil, Causey, Chance, Chapman, Choate, Clark, Clayton, Cloud, Clubb, Cochran, Cole, Collier, Collins, Conner, Cope, Coward, Cox, Crane, Cravey, Crawford, Cullers, Cunningham, Dalton, Daniel, Davidson, Davis, de Beauchamp, de Brueys, Deatherage, DeGarmo, Dennis, Deville, Dickerson, Dodd, Dozier, Draper, Duncan, Earp, Eaton, Edge, Edwards, Elliott, England, Epperson, Etheridge, Faircloth, Fargason, Faulk, Ferguson, Flowers, Foddrell, Ford, Formby, Fortenberry, Foster, Fowler, France, Frazier, Gailey, Garner, Garrett, Gilbert, Glass, Gorden, Gordon, Graham, Gray, Gregory, Griner, Grubb, Hale, Hall, Hammond, Harlan, Harper, Harris, Harrison, Henry, Herring, Hicks, Hill, Hodges, Hoffman, Holland, Hooks, Hopkins, Hudson, Ice, Isbell, Ivey, Jackson, James, Jenkins, Jett, Jones, Jordan, Keith, Kelley, King, Kirkland, Lacy, Lane, Leslie, Lewis, Marshall, Martin, McCoy, McDaniel, Mills, Mitchell, Morris, Neville, Odom, Owen, Pate, Payne, Perkins, Pinkard, Pitts, Ponthieu, Prather, Puckett, Pyle, Qualls, Reece, Ritenour, Rose, Rushing, Sanders, Seabolt, Seale, Sellers, Seybold, Slocombe, Swearingen, Talley, Terwilliger, Thomas, Thrasher, Trotti, Underwood, Van Den Berge, Van Ness, VanDeventer, Vaughan, Vincent, Wakefield, Waller, Watts, Welch, Whipple, Whittington, Wiess, Woolsey, Wynn, Yarbrough, Yates, Yocum, Yongue, Younger, Zabriskie, Zellers, Zuercher

About the Author

Gary L. Morris worked from 2009 to 2014 as a professional researcher for a major player in the genealogy field. After tracing his family lineage back to 1683, he found that genealogy could be an expensive undertaking. As such, has decided to publish these helpful guides to share the valuable free information he has discovered during his career to help others trace their family lineages as inexpensively as possible. An avid genealogist himself, he hopes you will find this guide factual, thorough, helpful, and most of all, effective in helping you to find your family members.

Notes

Notes

www.ingramcontent.com/pod-product-compliance
Lightning Source LLC
Chambersburg PA
CBHW061930280526
45787CB00004B/1555